MW01503307

FAR AND AWAY

Books by Mark Jarman

Tonight is the Night of the Prom
North Sea
The Rote Walker
Far and Away

FAR AND AWAY

Mark Jarman

Carnegie-Mellon University Press
Pittsburgh 1985

ACKNOWLEDGEMENTS

The Cumberland Poetry Review: Two Rivers,
Widow's Fire, While You Are Gone I Look for
Constellations
The Chowder Review: The Face of the Wave,
Classmates
The Hudson Review: Ideal Conditions, Poem in June
Kayak: Ballad of Larry and Club
The Missouri Review: The Medium
The New Yorker: Far and Away, The Supremes,
By-Blows, To the Reader, Cavafy in Redondo
The Ohio Review: Half Sonnets
Pequod: A Mackerel Sky
The Sonora Review: Caprices
Tar River Poetry: Last Easter
Threepenny Review: Poem for the Heartland
Water Table: Bees at the Tide Line
Yarrow: Long Stemmed Roses

"Two Rivers" is for Garrett Hongo; "Cargo Cults" is
for Vern Rutsala; "Classmates" is for Sandra McPherson;
"Ballad of Larry and Club" is for Robert McDowell;
"The Seawall" is for Charles Wright; "The Homing
Instinct" is for Jimm Cushing.

The publication of this book is supported by grants from the
National Endowment for the Arts in Washington, D.C., a
federal agency, and from the Pennsylvania Council
on the Arts.

Library of Congress Catalog Card Number 84-72534
ISBN 0-88748-008-X
ISBN 0-88748-009-8 Pbk.

Contents

For Amy

The earth is a wave that will not set us down.

I

FAR AND AWAY

For nights like this they forgot the continent.
Why they came or why their parents came
apparently always had to do with the weather.
They feel so much at home, air and skin match so perfectly,
is beside the point.
Here it is Santa Monica, July 4th,
and they pump from the open ends
of streets, clotting the cliff edges—friends,
families and loners, a sign of health.

The old ax head, America, cuts
under surf here, and what is real
or not turns abstract.
The night curves like a bandshell,
and if to light it up they attack
with fireworks, they can't budge
a thing but their own hearts.
The palms, the gazebos of graffiti—
Be Here Now!—you can imagine all the silly
trappings, as they look up and down at the dark.

Two hundred feet below, the beach is amber
in protective lights and fronts
the ocean's jeweler's velvet. The arc
of someone's Mexican bottle rocket faints,
after a twisting spurt,
ghost in a bubble chamber.
Then the big stuff clamors for all eyes,
leaves no gaps for gasping.
Flower, exfoliation turn into one
steady miracle of blazing faces.

There is an individual desire
among them to fire sky-high and rain
in *oohs* and *ahs* and vanish,
touching no one who could swear
the dissolving lace capping him was ash:

like the eye's voluptuous looking—just to see—
see what it's like and, scattered
after blossoming, grow
into one piece again, feel the flow
of identity, your very own, from foot to head.

On nights like this it's not acceptable
to cough with cold or shiver with irony
at your own home
or at the amusement of your family,
which you must pick up like a telephone
even if only to set it back in its cradle.
There they
stand at the edge night draws from,
releasing it bombed
and speckled with afterimages. The current theory

that their coast will drown,
crack off up to Arizona,
they believe only as a grand occasion
for combustion, redwoods, gas,
and each of them a survivor with the news.
Who wouldn't want to be there then?
Think of the Pacific on that night,
like a deceptive Spanish dancing skirt
that shimmers and almost seems too short,
but when twirled flares out and fills your sight.

THE SUPREMES

In Ball's Market after surfing till noon,
we stand in wet trunks, shivering
as icing dissolves off our sweet rolls
inside the heat-blued counter oven,
when they appear on his portable TV,
riding a float of chiffon as frothy
as the peeling curl of a wave.
The parade m. c. talks up their hits
and their new houses outside of Detroit
and old Ball clicks his tongue.
Gloved up to their elbows, their hands raised
toward us palm out, they sing,
"Stop! In the Name of Love" and don't stop
but slip into the lower foreground.

Every day of a summer can turn,
from one moment, into a single day.
I saw Diana Ross in her first film
play a brief scene by the Pacific—
and that was the summer it brought back.
Mornings we paddled out, the waves
would be little more than embellishments:
lathework and spun glass,
gray-green with cold, but flawless.
When the sun burned through the light fog,
they would warm and swell,
wind-scaled and ragged,
and radios up and down the beach
would burst on with her voice.

She must remember that summer
somewhat differently, and so must the two
who sang with her in long matching gowns,
standing a step back on her left and right,
as the camera tracked them
into our eyes in Ball's Market.
But what could we know, tanned white boys,

wiping sugar and salt from our mouths
and leaning forward to feel their song?
Not much, except to feel it
ravel us up like a wave
in the silk of white water,
simply, sweetly, repeatedly,
and just as quickly let go.

We didn't stop either, which is how
we vanished, too, parting like spray—
Ball's Market, my friends and I.
Dredgers ruined the waves,
those continuous dawn perfections,
and Ball sold high to the high rises
cresting over them. His flight out of L. A.,
heading for Vegas, would have banked
above the wavering lines of surf.
He may have seen them. I have,
leaving again for points north and east,
glancing down as the plane turns.
From that height they still look frail and frozen,
full of simple sweetness and repetition.

THE FACE OF THE WAVE

I had a friend in that cottage industry
where my home listed to shore
among the kelp-snarl of alleys,
one of the boys who sculpted surfboards,
stoned on fumes of catalyzed resin
by late afternoon, painting brain cells blind,
knocking off when work skewed from his hands.

To him the wave was only a human horror,
abstract and heartless, to cross
just as it broke, like the breathtaking pelican.
A minor plain of gray shifting glass
might hollow out, building
a wall in one breath. As he rose,
folding himself into the wave, so I rose.

As simple as that, the friendship
that moved us, collapsing at last
as he did, balance and speech slurred.
He would slip, a leg go down to the knee
keeling the wave face, and his surfboard
kick its rail into his groin.
He used the calms to lie still.

Our last morning together,
fire in the Santa Monicas reached
an arm of smoke toward the bay
and sprinkled the beach with ashes.
He nodded asleep in the water.
The last word between us as friends
was a groan of recognition.

Our wave rode out from under us.
Afterwards, he leaned this way and that
on a crooked staff of driftwood
along the esplanade, or poked among
tide pools, his sun-whitened hair

and leathery tan misleading,
agèd at only sixteen.

And when he came back from that death,
at first I didn't know him,
the fresh young witness in class
whose tongue God freed
so it swelled with Old Testament damnations
under the filmy mercy of the New.
He was pale but still surf-lean.

And his hands, it was said—
always folded on desk or Bible—could heal.
We had much to say to one another
and never said it. In my yearbook,
the words of a rote scripture
and his name signed below
curve smoothly with their good news.

I read them—and remember one day
when I crouched at a tide pool
where I had seen him. Light plumbed
the lining of mouths and shields and stroked
a trapped bonita, stirring the atmosphere,
doubling and troubled.
Sea anemones flinched and retracted.

The tide would return to scoop out the fish,
but that day I saw my friend's talent,
circling and cramped in its hollow,
as I now see his escape, the transforming
rescue, as I believe he must see it,
from such things as trouble people
who think waves break like the heart.

LONG STEMMED ROSES

Mist clings tonight,
   and the hiss of passing cars
is like the release of pressure
   as pressure builds,

as Jody Portillo's Riviera
   trails his entourage
into the gym parking lot,
   his first name laced in the rear window . . .

Everyone was dancing—our girls
   wore their orchids,
the purple spotted horns,
   on their breasts.

And Jody's car club and their dates
   held roses in locked hands,
pumping a locomotion
   into the red petals.

Noise of rock, and outside,
   muffled hammers shattered glass,
and the Pacific Ocean
   breathed its fog.

Everyone was dancing,
   sheen of black hair and blonde,
smell of overfragrant colognes
   with songlike and brutal names.

Albums embalm such nights,
   and this one, too, scrawled
by cop light on parchment carbon
   has kept:

The girls standing apart,
   brown and white, doused

in the sulfur glare
  of the street lamps.

And the football team, huddled
  incongruously, breaking
with a bright shout.
  And the car club ready . . .

I remember the scent
  of low tide, Jody Portillo nicked
under the left nipple
  and the first string center in the thigh,

and feel the thorn on the stalk
  leading back to such
blossoms of memory,
  when we were young.

BY-BLOWS

They wake like opening sea anemones,
although none turns into a flower—
wake with their dew, a salt clamminess
on gritty skin, under the pier.
Above them, boards thump, panels unlock,
food machines cough. The gaunt morning moon
(Why should they look?) turns blue in the jowl.
From the surf I would watch them climb
the nubbled walk to the library park—
watch the sun accept if not bless them
as they rose, hung over on cough syrup
or pop wine—where bladed cacti filled
with sprinkler water, and certain benches
were somewhat safe. Told to move on,
there was the library, the nook tables
and pillowing books, and after a decent interval
the discreet voice that spoke.

What did my father tell me? About that one
who whirled to face a soaped window
as we passed on the bare avenue?
They blow into town, beg money, blow out again.
But you know the rest of it.
They taste sand every morning, wake
in flannel grayed with their sweat,
touch the tide's cold hem, and smell the sunrise.
Planting their fingertips, they can tell
a story as roundabout as any medieval allegory,
with their damp gunpowder stubble,
their drain-waste of hair,
their air of illegitimate princes
double-crossed by sires and stars.
What we see looking at them is what they see
looking away—the otherness of the moon,
which we feel no urge to correct.

BEES AT THE TIDE LINE

Have they been noted and disregarded,
sick of a life of sweetness?
One would be an exception
but now I expect them, wings limp,
digging, it seems, in the drenched sand.
For salt? But they are saturated
with salt. Iceplant blooms,
hanging thickly along the cliffs.
Have they been dragged down here
heavy with pollen? Greed, is it that simple?
Or overwork? Or age?

It was the gold
lighting wet shells,
rocks bursting with spray,
floral shirts and froth,
white caps in a wide bed.
It focused flight,
promised harvest,
the yellow bread and nectar,
not this numb mud of panic,
all the flowers elsewhere.

When I think I will write as truth
some fearful symmetry,
I remember the story of the port town
where stillborn children resembled
their longshoreman fathers, holding
in both hands, like a hawser,
the cord looped around their necks.
There was no genetic relationship.
We know it was merely chance.

The bee wears a Tartar overcoat
and the Tartar loves honey
and the taste of the sea.
He rides seeking

the place where bees die.
His horse hooves silence
the warnings of priests
to hold mystery in the mind's eye alone.
Ahead the surf
spreads its prayer rug.
The dark sand swarms and hums.

Ahead I find the agile
vanishing of the sand fleas
and the pipers drilling after them.
At the crotch of the loud wash,
iceplant on a fallen chunk of cliff
covers the narrow blow hole.
Spray salts the red flowers
and there are bees. Soon the tide,
as if it needed the crevice
to breathe with, will reach up
and one or two will drown,
the rest rising free.

What is the singular?
What we look at long enough
to see it blossom as it disappears.

TWO RIVERS

He rows up the great gutter of the river,
his breath and the fog both scented,
whiskey and gasoline. The concrete banks, obscured,
At intervals echo his stroke, his breathing.
the freeways put columns in his path,
beavered with flood trash, black and brown meshes
and gemlike scraps of chrome.
The wide bed is grooved for a streak of water.
How he navigates, it's impossible to say.

He's back out in the sun, oars shouldered,
mere balsa paddles varnished with cheap sap,
amputated from a park canoe.
His breath still reeks. He hitches home,
stops at the Beachside Fox
to scoop free popcorn, goad the timid usher.
Head bobbing, he describes his voyage,
the great Los Angeles flickering
like a film strip below the long-necked palms.

It's easy not to believe him. Where he lived
beside the wharf, the coral cluster of rooms
is gone, the Beachside Fox is gone,
and so is he—absences sewn shut
by the real river, the one that matters.
On Saturdays the boys on stingrays flooding
from urban centers, all morning to the piers,
dodging the pilings of the overpasses,
then returning into twilight,
have the right idea. Flow
with the traffic. Follow it.

THE MEDIUM

Perhaps solitude and loneliness,
like the ether, are connectives,
and the Negro on Melrose Avenue
carrying a mattress rolled
like a giant manuscript
and whispering a story
is heard in Paris. At a bar,
small glass of Côte du Rhone untouched,
a pale clerk raises his fixed gaze.

If so, the dead must listen, too,
driven mad or never bored.

When the past snaps open
like a paper sack, and the air
in your own lungs fills it,
you want to duck or justify old pain,
and feel the birth
of the small town mutterer,
the auto-conversant of the major city.
You want to speak, but don't,
yet they speak all the time.

Maybe here I'm speaking for myself.
Alone, you talk about other things.

Climbing in an Alpine train
through matted fields,
I sat knee to knee with a woman,
breathing in her cigarettes.
As passage, she showed her state medical card,
then bowed her head,

burnt lips mumbling something
translated as smoke. She knew a stranger
and pressed her knees away.

Her words were for someone else.
Maybe for you, or for us. Here, now.

CARGO CULTS

Wait for the arm to come back gold,
for the voice torn by vodka—
a meadowlark briared in quavering—
to regain its amplitude.
Simple enough the degeneration
of the will to a nagging wish.
Pray for the prognathous growth
of the child's face to sweeten,
for X amount of dollars as the month
is hooked like a baby's blanket
dragged off by a cat's paw.
A cold night. Yet the mercury rises
under a sheet of foam.
A hull grinds wedged in sand,
the load heavy, the bulwarks tilting
to our hands. We board,
our limbs bare, our desires bare,
winding among the decks, a tropism
of reward, intertwining of clutch and embrace.

When I heard of the cargo cults, I looked west.
I thought it was here they waited,
on the common shore of our town—
a town declining to a strip
of crumbling beach and a wreck
dim with flies on the far point.
And now they hid in their houses
as average as anybody,
as a boy hearing a name
that identified nothing he had known.
There was the Greek wreck where grain
was eaten by vermin, and beyond it
the gray bulk of the island,
two shapes like sisters
against the tea-stained horizon.
Nothing else, but the idea
of gathering on some undated holiday

with suitcases and shopping carts,
rich as grunion, slippery and escaping.

And if it were true; if this were the place
to wait for elaborate vessels
by sea or sky, laden with all
you desired or would learn to desire;
if all that was pale, hidden
half-blind and anemic,
would bronze with satisfaction;
if the signal fires of dawn
would set the island alight,
and the sails of the argosy,
there and there, would yearn toward us—
it was little enough we wanted.
Only money until the end of the month.
Only warmth around the baby
all night as we slept.
Only the talents like creatures torn
in the fields of the past.
Only the child's face to sweeten.
Only the arm to come back gold.

II

CLASSMATES

Where no one is native, even the waves
live by arriving and leaving,
and growing up is all vacillation.
Is the town like the ocean, the ocean the town?
Both spread farther than their horizons.
To put a root down, drive down
a piling into water-quick sand
and have it hold, what do you do?
I knew a girl who sang.
Her childhood passed as a cluster
of clock-strokes on her metronome.
When she found her bouquets,
she could have emerged from anywhere.
I knew another who wrote.
She heard knobs twist and felt the sun
crack her blinds and pull.
Aiming at sound and light,
she fired a shot that tugged her away.
I will explain. When waves are your citizens
(your only citizens), though you fill
with new complexes and strangers,
all are expendable. They spend themselves.
They break, are broken, and spread as far
as they can beyond a firm band of horizon.

Here are two in a beach town
on the rim of Los Angeles
with a tremor now and then
and the stint of smog, but a generous climate
and the limitless daily ocean—
yet they lock themselves in their rooms.
One fleshes her voice and body,
eating between solfeggios.
The other types her life—all fiction—
every day's searing sequence
bundled up for her teacher's desk.
He knows their gifts. He calls them

his singer, his writer, shaking his head.
Both are pale as windowshades.
One is rumored on the strand at night
but, so he thinks, looking for stories.
The other is even more secret,
humming in class to herself
but to him dull as a driveway.
High school ends; they disappear,
his writer into a final rumor
of family estrangement, drugs, a cult,
and his singer with her passing grade
after an awkward bow at his door.

They disappear? No, he disappears—
another onlooker, like all of those
who stay when living is leaving.
The singer makes music her health,
her sun and her meat, padding
her hips and her dressing rooms
with nights of growing applause.
The writer softens in a grip
a critic might call bad influences,
judging her life like her work—
a mawkishness here, there a banality,
a sense that nothing concrete
takes the print of her life,
the way above her hometown
the ceiling of yellow smog absorbs
the white smoke of the power plant.
In fact, she digs through the page
to another world and broods there,
but appears to be dancing,
joined in a ring with others,
planting feet in a floor of sand
in the shadow of a desert overhang, slowly
crowding herself in a stale cave,
waiting for her fame, too.

When they come—the American ends

of success and failure—we seek
the practice room and the hideout.
What happened there? Do we know?
As the singer suns herself in praise,
fattens on it or diets, still
back at the start was a door
closed to wave-sound, sun-bath.
Good, it appears, the beginning was good.
But as the assassin points her gun
at the unreal public man
who is suddenly alive and suddenly real—
back at the start is a door
closed to wave-sound, sun-bath.
Bad, it appears, the beginning was bad—
for this one. That is an answer,
if there are beginnings
and not, instead, a series of ends.
As for the teacher, he ends by hearing
"Tell my story," and never answers.
And at the great debut of his singer,
after the full vowels and ovations,
his backstage note is returned, a questionmark
jotted in greasepaint over his name.

So that is one story.
I end with another, naming waves
as accessories or foils
that glint at the eye corners for anyone
who lives by the ocean or leaves it.
For all their beauty, clumsy or poised,
their monotony must be oblique.
You cannot count every one.
Five years from home, the day I returned
at the end of summer, the Pacific
had a breath of desert heat.
I waded out among silver schools
in the tooled, temperate swells. They broke,
lifting my body in white arms
onto the sand. I knew this was home

and home was heaven. Then I started to count
the days, the waves, and to save myself
turned the corner of my eye only
to the daily surf. I expect their faces—
these women, girls where I was a boy,
long since turned away from there—
their faces would go blank.
We live in a landlocked country,
passing between our cells and stages.

BALLAD OF LARRY AND CLUB

The two old people chose my friends
   in sunny San Diego.
I played with them where the rainbow ends
   in balmy San Diego.

Grandmother favored the red-headed whip
   whose parents lived behind,
but Grandfather claimed that a friend with a chip
   on his shoulder was the right kind.

Larry would yawn in your face like a cat,
   then, with a sharp paw flick,
draw tears—never blood: a clever act.
   Larry showed leadership.

Club stared into the heart of light
   with patient, muddy eyes.
Club was slow, but his chief delight
   was catching Larry in lies.

Their houses could have been one house,
   same dead drifting smoke
laddering planes from their parents' mouths,
   same distance in the look

turned on their children by their mothers,
   same television eyes.
But knowing this about each other
   forged no loving ties.

My grandparents thought it a cozy combe,
   their sunburnt sunken street.
And during my summers it was home—
   black asphalt, white concrete.

During my visits, the summer months
   were spent in two kinds of play:

quiet with Club or brilliant stunts
   with Larry leading the way.

On a ridge above the neighborhood
   the eucalyptus bowed;
it was far from an enchanted wood,
   but it served for Larry's crowd.

Larry, high on the shaggy scent
   of eucalyptus and power,
made each of us climb as high as he went,
   near the dinner hour.

Larry would say his dad could crush
   a beer can flat as a quarter;
Larry would whisper—and the gang would hush—
   that his mom was a nun's daughter.

And Club, self-banished, overheard
   sometimes below the trees,
and said aloud, "Your dad is a turd
   like mine, and your mom's diseased."

Then Larry would have to descend the height
   of the eucalyptus tower
and face Club in the angled light
   near the dinner hour.

Club would shrug—big boy for his age—
   and show Larry his back
and walk away, as if at the last page
   he closed the book *thwack*.

The punches that Larry never threw,
   the things he should have said,
echoed among his quiet crew,
   echoed in Larry's head.

But if any boy, among us few,

asked Larry why he balked,
he would smile, "'Cause he's bigger than you."
That's how Larry talked.

Summers passed. My last one there,
   Grandmother was dying.
And grandfather, slumped in his easy chair,
   if he wasn't drinking was crying.

I wasn't missed the hours I spent
   on the floor of Club's bedroom
putting puzzles together, but sensed
   a funny kind of gloom.

It seeped with his parents' boozy smell
   and the dust riding the light
into Club's room and into himself.
   Even there, it wasn't right.

One day I knocked on Club's front door.
   It opened with a rap.
I found him sitting on the living room floor
   with something in his lap.

He sat spread-legged on the carpet stain
   made by the morning sun.
His eyes were fixed on the magazine
   of a Korean vintage M-1.

"At breakfast," he said, not looking up,
   "there was nothing good to eat.
Dad's butts were in a coffee cup.
   Mom picked at her feet.

"I looked outside at the sunny sunshine
   coming straight down like rain.
I thought about your folks and mine.
   I could see it like a scene

out of a movie, how sad they were
   to live in this dead-end gulley,
that you get to leave at the end of summer.
   And, of course, I thought about Larry."

He pulled the bolt back and I asked,
   "Where did you get that gun?"
I tried to laugh the way Larry laughed,
   and then a voice said, "Run."

Out in the street a football twirled
   and seemed to hang in the sky,
the leather star of that little world.
   Someone yelled, "Let me try!"

I broke into Larry's circle of fun,
   out of breath and weeping.
Before the first shots, he had everyone
   swept with him into hiding.

Of all the rounds that Club got off
   his last morning alive
only one was aimed well enough.
   The rest of us survived.

My grandmother, too, who lived to see
   her husband die of the grief
he'd uncorked the summer he thought that she
   would precede him to the grave.

And at her funeral I stood
   with Larry and his daughters,
recalling it all—for ill or good—
   with the arrogance of survivors.

A DAILY GLORY

When he told it later, he would say,
"Once, I was not what I am now.
A woman changed me, a miracle.
I worked the day-shift along the beach,
the pier-rat, one-man, stinking-dead-fish squad,
which ended at the hilltop library park.
I carried a pamphlet of nude girls,
pure porn, but it was like smelling
a strong odor to mask another.
I saw things rotting, stinks clung.
I'd sneak glances, suck a peppermint.
I could read minds like morning weather,
like the flocking of flies, but couldn't
read her mind. She offered it so freely.
Easy enough when the photographed face
above the body pretends willingness
or offers a thrilling detachment, hating you.
A mind being read lets you handle it,
but hers, part coral, part quicksilver,
part so many parts it came apart, said,
'You mustn't drift as books let you,
following a phrase to sleep.'
And it was a stronger mask than nudes
and hard candy. I left myself
among the tidal corpses, the tourist garbage.
I began to see, despite the clinging.
Grained in my skin like sea tar was a reek
she registered, as mild as I grew, as sweet,
that fell between us as the space we stood,
two squares apart on the library walk.
I'd be busy with the hose, the gulls begging,
or neatening the flare-ends in my cart,
that chaperone of stewing pier trash,
slick and beachy, ripening in the sun.
I kept my pictures separate.
Why would I flaunt them, dingy tickets
to nowhere she'd want to go?

But I explained my system, said at dawn
I had to go to hell, and took
a burlap sack and flashlight
into the sticky air below the pier,
and tried to strike the dead things
before I smelled them. Fish, mere troughs of worms;
gulls limply compact, gray wings that
I kept from flapping open as I bagged them;
and the pier rats, men and animals,
sleeping, sometimes dead.
The pilings stepped back into rock and sand.
I poked the cave with my light,
a yellow brush, and called it quits,
cuffs wet, hands marked, sack bleeding,
my whole body heavy with the odor.
She said she knew. She knew how things
wax sickly and cling. Carnations came to her mind,
funeral flowers, how years before
her mortician boyfriend smelled of them.
He had seen in hers a compatible profession.
Could he feel as she felt about her books,
as if he owned the body he had dressed?
She wanted to tell me what it was like to have
that clinging—the knowledge that he could."

How fine to lead an exemplary life,
each gesture a template rising from the page,
white and black as ink on paper, radiant.
People not only want to read it,
they want to live it. Your breakfast.
Your dissatisfactions, rages, compromises.
Your nightly swoons into sleep.
Your life is like the sunlight on a hilltop
where pilgrims heal themselves . . .
A bridge crumbles, falling into ice,
tinder snaps into bits for the fire—
pages are turning. Everyone, even the drunks
who bask in the window nooks, is reading.
Out the window the elemental pool speaks

as it is spoken to. Waves nod.
Their necks break. Correct. Gull cries
go soft as dust, flour of preservation.
The barbered garden shows the care
of the afternoon attendant. "I'm a reader,"
it might say sympathetically.
"Yeah, I love to read." And there he is,
as ignorant as any of it,
his glossy photos rolled in his palm.
She stops in the back stacks, at a window
barred with downy black against the sun.
Just under her hand his crab grass hair
pokes up as he twists a hose cap tight.
A star of leakage shoots wet beams.
"Stupid spigot." He wipes his face.
His hose prints halfmoons on the wall
behind shrubs. Fading, they seem to set.
A patina grows on his photographs of girls.
He's sick of their slick flatness,
the phony moisture of his thumbs across
their skin, the image of their skin,
the image of the image of their skin.
He wants to talk. "That's all," he says.
"I want to talk." She has entered
the sky pasted up in his head, moving for him
as only an image can, more line than flesh.
She knows and does not recoil.
Among the purposeless in the fiction shelves,
the knights of the road who could reach up
and have their own stories in hand,
she forgives from the deep well of a book.
"He was the worst, but it was all trappings.
We can't forgive men their trappings.
He decked himself with the worst, but traveling
into that shabby jungle of women's bodies,
I reached that look scored by errors
and wiped them away like cataracts.
It isn't always so. Most turn into what adorns them,
leers and wet-looking posters.

40

That afternoon I went with him, at the door
he said, 'You might not like it here.'
I knew what I'd have to face—the nudes
like pier glasses, the put-together puzzles,
the projector pointing at the screen.
My stomach clenched and dropped.
He offered food. He called, 'I knew
you wouldn't like it.' He stood outside his door,
'I thought you wanted to see where I lived.'
We could see the ocean beyond the flexing surf,
looking back ingenuously, unlike us.
The concrete steps rang under my feet,
the banister echoed. I stopped.
'I'm sorry,' he said, and I said, 'Yes, you're sorry.'
The unruffled breeze ruffled me. I smelled change.
Spring held, but there is always change here
from good to better weather, from best
back to a daily good, fog lifting by noon.
It was the out-tide leaving its odor to us.
All that gurry and decay wafting in
as a sweet brininess on the breeze.
I decided it was a good thing.
I watched as the projector blew like a heat duct.
Dust clung to light. The paid flesh mingled.
Pure as the corner of the sofa where he hunched,
he watched. I was safe as milk at a boozer's picnic.
I watched all he cared to show, thinking odd
how some constructed plots, then saw the one of me.
Quivering, inexact, I was leaving work,
new books like a baby on my hip.
I looked to the side, yes,
looking for him, then flickered forward.
He must have been near the parking lot,
under the honeysuckle. I strode past
and ended the film as shins and feet.
No plot, but the plot that placed me there.
The light came up like memory that won't be
flinched from. 'I want to change,' he said.
'That's what I want.' Under the pier, I knew

even the glassy sand rots, and in the library,
leaves of paper survive the fall,
some bending only so far. I recalled
the bouffant hag who caught me, a child,
whipping through the dictionary there.
Licking her thumb, like an ice cream cone,
and motioning me, tongue out, to do the same,
she led me through the flimsy, translucent pages.
I felt that royal gesture—hag
that I may be or even am—that reaches
to hold the ugly creature and kiss it.
I took the man in my arms, a clutch
of quirky lines, and I changed him."

CAPRICES

At your window the sea obeyed.
You returned to the broken glass,
the rag you ripped methodically,
and so to yourself. More

than the sea, your vision obeyed
and your lack of vision.
Where did it stop? The rag
in uneven strips on the tile,

rack of dishes dripping,
glass blade flat in
the agile fold of your hand.
Where did you continue?

You opened your eyes to the good
color rising in the world's
faces, all of which turned to you,
smiled, and turned away.

*

You had gone far ahead simply
by what I had not touched, by light
I had not struck. But you cried
not to meet you, cried
till I took you to bed, with lights out,
your eyes against my thick shoulder.

*

At the stone trough in the pasture,
among poppies, your fingers
curled on the rim white and fast as dead ivy.
I pointed to mud with twin
leaf prints of deer. Without looking,

you acknowledged, standing in another night
by a lawn of ice tipped toward you,
as if your face compared
to the lesser whiteness of the stars,
the frost, the isolated house,
were a legacy
from which without fail, wisely,

the deer flee.

*

At task after task I discover
the word or look that would have saved you.
It drops and scurries into a crack.

The window reveals me to the night.
I darken this side
to see the real darkness, which is paler,

so that your pain shows
to its best advantage,
one branch reaching forward through thousands of leaves.

LOST IN A DREAM

When I drove the L. A. canyon with the dead cat
in three Chinese boxes in a garbage bag,
the eucalyptus hedges like rows of embassies
and the sun diplomatic and the radio on for its voice,
its cool, odorless voice counseling love—to a beat—
up ahead, bees pranced obsessed with a queen,
drunk on the formic in their stingers.
I heard the rock at Madame Ling's the night we dressed
as if ties knotted right would annex us a home.
The singer wore triangular sunglasses, had starred as a child
in ads for kiddie medicine. He bounced up and down.
And his mom matched him spasm for spasm; dad, too.
It was the music of home and we had come back,
planning to do more than dance, but we couldn't stay.
Late, as we left, a bald giant appeared
with a life-sized doll in a box under his good arm.
With his teeth, he ripped the cellophane window open
and called for Madame Ling, to give her his gift.

As the bees descended, I saw the pet shelter
and the quivering air above its incinerator
and rolled up my window, thinking the cat's death
would not sweeten the teeth of these fat bees.
We had lain in bed that morning, our baby 10-days-old,
and tried to bless our leaving like our home.
When Persian jasmine mingled with gasoline
and the sun, like a piece of bait, stained the ocean
and the canyon crows blew past as if cut
from cathedrals of black paper, and rolling tremors
sailed our bed at dawn toward the horizon,
we had no explanation for what we felt.
Outside our window, the cat returned
and stretched out with its right hip laid open.
Its fur had been the color of hearth-fire.
Its dog-faithful gait had followed from room to room.
We lay in bed, talking, sensing only
the satisfying taste of our native salt.

First, the cat's cold body shocked us, then
the pale gash that kindled black ants
out of the damp clay-and-sand soil,
then, it was the tongue clenched as always—
kittenish—at the tip between his front teeth.
We had imagined it would redden the baby's cheek.
Who would tear us out of this box of a day?
But we had to leave. We had a year and a child.
Circumstance like instinct pointed away.
I drove slowly, the pelting rain of bees
glanced off the windshield, the music beat
the dashboard grid over the radio speaker,
and rising from the shelter chimney, the column of mirage,
the sort of air that paradise must rest on,
straightened the bent eucalyptus—those trees
so delicious in honey, so tart in the blood
that natives carry their blue-green fruit into exile.
We had to leave. This death would see us off.

That day is nailed in place by that chimney.
After the bees cleared, after I dumped
the odd coffin into white-coated arms,
I wanted to flow back down to the beach,
collect you and the baby and head out to sea
or cling like sand to the agate-webbed rocks
where we had walked every evening throughout the pregnancy.
The banked houses would catch the sunset
in wide, complacent windows as we climbed
up from the beach every evening as if toward
a room we knew with our eyes closed,
the simple need to find another home.
At night, the cat would listen at your belly,
hearing a purr as deep as his own. Deeper.
And when he returned outside our bedroom window,
having dragged a surprise of blood through the garden,
he heard the baby snuffling and sputtering
and heard us saying, "What a year this has been."

III

HALF SONNETS

I want to leave absence where I find it,
not enter absence—how is that possible?
Could we, the semicircle staring up
like lambs and shepherds dazzled by a star,
go inside the oval opening
of the girl from childhood's cleft palate?
If so, no messages would come back.

*

I would take your place, give you mine,
but that would be half the story.
There is no mystery in temperatures
when yesterday the wasps fanned their wings,
those smoked glass snippets, and today
swarm toward any chink, high window, eave
in order not to freeze. Who would be one?

*

You have said that you would take
the whining in my ears, the dull
side of my tongue, and limping speech,
if I could only sleep
and say that I was happy as I am,
now, changed. Your body takes mine
and makes another body. We're the same.

*

If diminishment is, finally, necessary,
where do the wasps winter, which ones last?

The white paper capsules
turn grayer daily with an inner frost.
During August they emerged complete,
so complete, the black stripes, mustard eyes,
like grown-ups with jobs and personal tastes.

*

I love you more than my work. I hold
within my mouth, like the ball of pulp
pinkish and damp in their jaws
that the wasps work into paper—
in my mouth I hold the words
all worked together to turn perfect.
I love you more and say, that, too, to work.

*

I mentioned her, the child who owned a hole
she shouldn't have, a vacancy framed
with membrane lit by her open mouth
for a crowd of children, illuminated by our wonder,
because that cloud of paper
glued at two points to the window is so
like it and unlike it. She was healed.

*

We wanted to be one another and ourselves,
to tell each other exactly at first
of the first pleasure of lovemaking.
We chewed the luster from our illustrations,
working so hard we softened and let up,
living inside the limits once again,
the healed need of more than our sore skin.

*

Perfect palate or flawed, roof or empty
beams under blazing clouds and moon,
partition that hints the universe
is two halves like the body though is not.
The hint is what the yearning's for—
to be other, other and yet still
alive inside never to return, oneself.

*

Mitosis, and we are a household.
The baby rocks, a continent of growing cells.
All that we had wanted just to be,
synthesis, dialectic in the chubby flesh.
More whole than we and less and not to be shaken
yet, abandoned to the rattling cold like paper.
All we wanted, made, to be never completely known.

WIDOW'S FIRE

At the hour when homeowners
stroll out to ponds and rose beds,
we come here, the new tenants,
to the bottom of her yard
to the circle of ashes
where light inflaming the stems
of the bordering pokeweed
repeats an auto-da-fé.
We try to make them fit,
the black branches mortared down
by strips of yellow moss,
the souvenir plate's palm trees
unscorched and green on its shards,
the dim thighs of the nudes
on charred wedges of magazine,
the cindery house keys
in the changed locks of the house,
thinking grief or spite or both,
of her piled up whorls of hair
aging under blonde rinses
and her eyes' martyred look
when she comes for rent and sees
the whole house still containing
so much she could have burned.
She scares us both, talking fire
insurance, faulty wiring,
the furnace blazes of winter,
offhandedly, "part of life",
till we lie open in bed
to the fear of fire closing
our throats and the baby's room
and return here to these clues.
So little really, so small,
the fragments, the arrayal,
that the misery she meant
to burn seems a mere subset
of a greater misery

which includes the colored wreaths,
Christmas ghosts in the attic,
and the zoo of bric-à-brac
boxed in the cellar shadows
and the memory of them
or the fatigued disregard
that spared them and built only
a small fire of a few things.
The branches must have been fuel
and the skin magazines, too,
but the crockery and keys
are such raw invitations
and clearly not for strangers,
it is hard not to conclude
that nobody really died.
What he shook off in leaving
was hers to burn, and she burned
just enough to show him that.
As light drains from the pokeweed
it seems the greatest misery
might be a great happiness
that in order to burn it all
so little has to be burned.
That is this evening's theory.
Growing older we need one
just to sleep, every night,
a new one just to sleep.

WHILE YOU ARE GONE I LOOK FOR CONSTELLATIONS

It is chaos at first,
which it truly is,
these fossil lights
of flyaway stars,
then the charts
under my flashlight
begin to match
what I see. Backwards
at first, the Pleiades
appear west, and then I see,
and turn to Deneb,
the Swan's tail,
and the Swan angling
toward the earth.
In an hour of craning
I have it down,
the cold clings
like a coat of mail.
I name Vega, Altair,
and laugh as I have since childhood
when finding out answers.
Over my shoulders
Orion lugs, on his shoulder,
the giant Betelgeuse
coming after the faint Sisters.
Never has he caught up,
though that axial star
in Cygnus, diving for cover,
looks like a wound.
Never have I missed
you as I do. I walked
all day through the house
into the small town,
checked out this text
on astronomy for the cover
packet of star charts

and waited for night,
the darkest clearest part
and the longest part
when these stars were
first named in places
which they have long since left.

POEM IN JUNE

My daughter is riding out after rain
    in the undercast light of sunset
    when the great ash a block away,
    studded with grackles like fleas,
turns, for an instant, a color worth
a long meditation on heartbreak. I stop,
    and, astride my shoulders, she gasps
    and sinks fingers into my hair.

So I save the speech I might have made
    to my two-year-old daughter,
    saying instead, "Look at the tree.
    How many black birds?"
and feel the root-tearing grip in my hair relax
as she trusts me again and responds, "Look at it!
    How many black birds!" I count,
    rolling my shoulders to steady her.

And she trills the numbers off her tongue
    and keeps counting, looping ahead and back.
    Sequence is a thread of grass,
    and the years before she was born
and the years she will outlive her parents
and be herself outlived, can be woven to make,
    however tangled, one network
    of time to hold this moment.

So an odd slant of light turns a tree
    of new leaves the color of fall; three birds
    perch there, like an October day.
    So today, thirty, I can say
how long it takes to grow up. When she is ready,
as children do, she will decide how I lived.
    Now she is riding, and for her,
    as she cups my ears and points my face,

I am a good horse. At the oily creek,

I watch for fat water moccasins
and set her down at the edge.
I claw rocks from mud
and she pitches them sidearm, underhand, in chance arcs.
They land at her feet, clattering on shingle.
And they hit home, splashing crowns
briefly clear from the black surface.

IDEAL CONDITIONS

If I can count the levels
  that hover under the pond's green ceiling—
   quick fingerlings and minnows
   and the thicker presences
that part them, rising through the clouds of my scratched lenses,
   turning their spotted flanks,
  enormous in that room, and scattering
    the small like dust in the sun,
then lowering themselves back into the plush mud;

   if I can pinch the wings
  of the swooning dragonfly whose blue length
   pulses once and hangs,
   wings that seem laced with soot,
and do it with my butcher's hands like a cat,
   and pierce its crisp thorax
  with a hook as fine as a mounting pin
   and, when it strikes, separate
the perch from the bait, both perfectly intact;

   if I can catch a scent
  not meant for me, some molecule
   in code, an old agreement
   between two that I might startle,
following the bee and pulling back the petal,
   and recognize the source
  under the webbed cornice of honeysuckle,
   and look up toward the house
and feel that you will step outside any moment;

   if, already alert
  within the bars of insect sound,
   that cage of summer heat,
   I can focus on your voice
burning its sweetness into the shrill noise
   so that, unaware,
   you walk out into the lush weather

singing but already there—
if I can imagine song and make you appear;

    then I know what I am—
    a soul with all windows open.
    The world framed in each,
    gossiping like a neighbor,
suddenly sucks in breath and can only gesture;
    still, I try to speak.
    Lavisher of the senses, angel,
    here is the place to make
your visitation. I can almost taste it.

TO THE READER

Today, having turned 83,
I turn back in my coma.
I see my last moment awake, erect.
Sun fills the empty piazza
crenelated by shadows of towers.
There is the first step of the flight
to the blank-faced duomo
and a sound of Sunday mumbling
amplified by open doors.
If I step forward, I am here,
jangled, drifting and stilled,
with a flashback of ambulance bells,
a huddle of nursing nuns,
faint Italian farewells.
So I step back and find
the reversal ironically clear,
dustless, rhythmical.
My clothes, difficult
all those years of old age,
turn smooth, slipping on thoughtlessly
like my own face in the mirror
and my wife's appearing beside it.
We have our whole past ahead of us.
Our children reattach
and like us grow younger
but more rapidly. They shrink
back to their births.
What is it like to lose them so?
Affection intensifies
inversely to their departures.
Soon so small, they hide
within their baby blankets.
Then birth is reversed.
My wife swallows
their pain and hers
and that pain and affection are gone
and we continue.

I understand the room-building
of marriage now,
as if the baroque could be picked apart,
broken arches rejoined,
rounded and then uninvented.
As we built we could separate,
work all day out of thought
of each other. Finally,
we are alone in one room;
the sexual sweetness is almost too much.
Then she vanishes.
How quick was our courtship.
How brief adolescent loneliness
that had seemed endless.
My childhood knots up again,
all of its strings and entwinings
just as enigmatic,
embowelled with codes, insinuations,
untying one by one.
Flat characters who are siblings
zip off like meteors.
Then, parents. I see four hands
knitting this carefully
to make a clear thing—

> But reader, within the hill
> of this city where I am dying
> are vaults of an ancient people.
> They undermine the city.
> A framework of steel
> has been built for support.
> Water flooding the vaults
> rusts the steel, more is added.
> The I-beams bristle
> inside the hollow crown.
> The city stands on its brittle base,
> a wall sinks, a tile courtyard cracks.
> We have reached a steady state
> of support and collapse

  like the human face—

not this ball of entanglements.
They gather me up.
And I am lost.
And it is not to death.

IV

THE SEAWALL

Palm Sunday. Nothing worse
than a cold Passion in Scotland.
Back after 20 years from California,
from palm fronds and hearts of palm,
to the treeless town of slate roofs.
In a week He rises again.
I walk the seawall dusted
by the North Sea's joint-rusting smoke.
Cloaking you once, it cannot
be oiled out of your bones.
What Mediterranean would enter this place,
treading on sprays of frost?

The seawall raises its own horizon.
I know what it means to hear
sympathy and impotent sighing,
the working of weak lungs, in the surf;
to see the dead pulled under the earthworks,
their white grasp slipping from rip rap;
and the sea coal scattered along the beach
like a trade for the poorest
who bend to it. There is always
a first sea of importance
that the second, like the Pacific,
could swallow with a pang of ice.

At the seawall's back, the maze of living.
A butcher shop stuffy with flesh odors,
its damp walls, porcelain cases.
A church where chalices are passed
dabbed by great handkerchiefs, like snow on armor,
their rims warmed by lips.
And my father's roses in the parsonage garden,
like overturned footstools, 20 years old,
49er, Texas Centennial, Newport News—
the tags lost, the black clods
roughened all over, glittering.

LAST EASTER

When the body rises, laboring,
    a startling green oblong
that flips on the line, drawing
    a crowd to the barge side,
you can hear the cheering,
    if the surf is quiet, even among
the eucalyptus hedges where
    trunks and falcate leaves,
all sun-clawed, shelter fighting
    and walking places and caked
rain ditches. You can hear it,
    a foam of beer and bait blood.
The barge itself is a vague patch
    by day, by night an *m* of lights,
and appears quite still always
    on its long chain to shore.
Last Easter when a storm turned it
    up on the beach, the muddy hull
reclined in the scrubbed sunlight.
    Heart's flesh bougainvillea
was turning to paper,
    and, as the wind departed,
the pyrocantha's flame-sterilized
    needles seemed to draw
across the huge cleanliness,
    tearing the water to cotton,
then mending and tearing it again.

    Even the cupboards of the barge's
concession stand were full
    of frightened fish.
As the tug pulled, out dumped
    waterfalls of bonita and anchovy,
like vaults of silver ingots,
    at the feet of those gathered.
Though not in church, they most likely
    believed that if a body rises,

it must pass through rock as through cloud
    or climb like the flounder
into an element of complete surprise.

    Beside the sea, resurrection
is in the blood, that inland sea,
    for the drowned come back
as dependably as the sand pared
    from agate shelves all winter creeps
back in spring. It's in the blood,
    or in the sacks the Cano brothers
carried home through the eucalyptus,
    elbowed and stomached with bonita,
and would drop at a flicked pebble
    to fight—when young with fists,
and finally with knives.
    That sea we hold within resurged
from their cuts as they died,
    and the ungutted fish swam
in the surprising element.
    Though the dead come back dead,
resurrection is that wanting out,
    the escape to transformation.

When the barge was saved and towed
    out to its anchorage, the cheering
and the grinding of sand and motors
    could be heard among
the eucalyptus, softened to an absent
    Aramaic, perhaps, that meant
"What's done is done." But tracking
    the sounds deeper inland, before

they faded, like a track of blood
   after the first vivid splash,
dribbling over and under the undergrowth,
   and ending in a vacant shaded place
where the creature pawed a bed,
   slept, then covered its spoor,
they might have said to some ears,
   "What is gone is gone."

POEM FOR THE HEARTLAND

Your landlocked blood beats, your eyes tear;
when told of a distant coast, you say it is not real.
It is real only here. The sea condensed
in blood, tears, salt is the real sea.
Word of another place comes like an oar
on a stranger's arm, a shovel to sift sand.

Where waves shake beds, the dreams that come,
bulky rollers molded by the ocean floor,
unfold like long novels full of characters
limned by breezes and nuances of foam.

You are right. A life of tides where seasons
change color in the water must be fiction.
But it can lock you in like winter,
if missing winter, that is what you desire.

IF I AM LIKE ANYTHING

When I was my father's child,
the days unravelled like a sweater.
Lamb's wool and the froth of beetles
spun sunlight into globes,
spirals, rods, all radiance.
I was his child out walking
the spring fields opening with mud.
The milch cows turned their steep faces
and knew me, the son of an engine.

My father was a fine invention.
He built the city and the night.
Even as I detect the green
catching from tree to tree on the field's edge,
and the frogs waking in flooded ditches,
and the paper wasp and the cabbage white
gnawing their way out,
wet, furled—I remember
the combustion of air, fuel, and a spark.

Others may tease a soul
from the red tail or the crows it sends,
scolding, to another grove.
Or capture the look the muskrat holds
when it freezes in the human presence.
In their presence, I feel his,
and know if I am like anything
it is one of those wheeling galaxies
that mesh without touching.

A MACKEREL SKY

Small, separate clouds, each
   in a blue socket,
collect in wide vees over
   the apricot tree-house.
A boy there plucks
   antennae from the butterflies
he calls orange skippers
   and releases, powdery rockets
spinning upwards, eaten
   by a mackerel sky.

It's the past. I saw it coming
   early this evening as
the clouds changed, and the broomstick
   sapling grew, and this desk—
temporary in my parents' house—
   broke into rough boards
nailed among leaves. My hand
   fits inside the child's,
feels the wings between thumb and index,
   and the slick dust.

And pulls away. Because I
   can't wrench him
from his work. It is the past.
   I'm only here to visit.
And, too, I know what's coming—
   the gray sheath that slides
below such high, white clouds; the rain
   that falls between the boy and me,
beyond which I can hear
   the branch crack and his cry.

THE CITY IN THE SEA

Coastal spring, desert spring,
the air a balm of weightlessness,
yet the students in their rows
as the light drapes their shoulders
are writing almost in unison.
My mother is among them.
When they pause,
the whole class trembles,
but I know her trembling.
One hand anchors a page,
the other copies.
This glimpse of my mother's past,
this suburb of Los Angeles,
what am I looking for?

To say the city is a net
is to number its strands
and exclude much.
To say a bed of kelp,
swelling and subsiding,
mazey with eels and sunfish,
says a little more.
It is a sea, too, and floods
my memory like a basin,
filling it with salt water,
its complexity, that will neither
quench thirst nor wash
without leaving its residue
but in the end sustains.

My mother's school, her apartment house,
even the post office
where her mother works,
are like aquarium sculpture.
One street binds them all
running below magnolias.
As I think of her, those trees

open and lose their flowers,
ancient, simple corollas.
A hand spreads wide a petal,
a fingernail engraves it.
The broad evergeen leaves
give their cold-blooded gleam.

I try to turn that look,
that simple, evergreen gaze,
on myself, too. One night,
leaving a plain, brick church
and some youth event behind,
I ran with my girlfriend
on that street, under the trees,
ending in the schoolyard
where we embraced and kissed.
We had come miles by car
and did not know where we were.
Though I touched her breast
and held her indignant stare,
we both kept kissing.

Why should it have mattered,
once I learned the coincidence,
to feel as if I had come
twenty years too late?
But I remember a story.
In a dream, a girl's drowned lover
speaks to her, two vague words.
Awake, pursuing him,
she boards a ship made of stone,
and as it sinks, becomes a sunfish.
She seeks him only to learn
her life has saved his,
and now they are both alone.

The two words were "your soul."
When I return to this city
I am always looking for something.

I believe my mother is writing,
in that imagined classroom,
the history of a word.
Old English, Dutch, German,
Old Icelandic, Gothic, *soul* related to *sea*.
Related, too, to the future
where she will tell me stories
like that one, and give me a soul,
believing—of course, believing—
that I will never lose it.

THE HOMING INSTINCT

There we see him, driving
the canyon's winding stem,
   from sea marsh
    through sweet real estate,
late in the afternoon.

   A huge doll
    frocked in yellow
sits beside him on the seat.
Her eyes rock open and look
   through cellophane.

She is a gift for Madame Ling
who sits beside the stage
   after the Island dancing
    in her restaurant
and lets the young bands play.

   The light peels
    from eucalyptus trees
and clusters in chaparral.
And suddenly a cloud of bees,
   dancing for a queen,

gilds the air. It rides
his radio's thumping pulse,
   a crazy rain
    of loyalty,
each note a little fury.

   Windows up,
    safe as the doll's
hard and rosy skin,
he nods in time to this music,
   and then it dies.

When he enters Madame Ling's,

strobed by the harsh silver
  as the bass begins,
  he will call for her
and try to catch her eye.

  Meanwhile the day
  recedes, and where
the canyon rises among
the freeways, he enters night.
  We see him there,

his face patched by passing lights,
his neck and shoulders thrusting
  back and forth
  to another beat
we faintly hear. We see him.

  We see the city
  let him take
its privacy, like a nectar,
and mix it with his nerves,
  and make it honey.

CAVAFY IN REDONDO

Our ruins run back to memory.
Stucco palaces, pleasure bungalows, the honeycomb
of the beachcombers' cluster of rentals—
I remember them, filings in sand
pricking up at the magnet of nostalgia,
a sigh of dusty filaments. Our ruins
wear the as-yet-unruined like coral crowns.
Night life blows through the boardwalk's
conch-shell coils of neon, skirting the water.
This was never—Ask my parents—a great city.
It had its charm, like a clear tidal shallows,
silted-in now, poldered, substantial, solid,
set for the jellying quake everyone expects.

I walked these streets one night with a new lover,
an as-yet-to-be lover—it took a whole night
of persuasion. I had been gone a year,
and walked as sea mist compounded the dew.
My legs ached by the time bed was agreed to.
How sentimental it was, to flatter, listen,
cajole, make little whining endearments,
plodding ritualistically among landmarks,
sandy shrines in alleys, the black meccas
of plate-glass windows fronting the beach
where white froth reflected in the night.
I kept that ache, not love's, after we parted.

We did not part to history with its glosses;
we were not even footnotes. Our ruins
will bear out no epics or histories here,
footprints compounded of dew and fog
and under them, maybe a rusty antique
that, boiled in acids, will tell a tale.
After all, ships passed, broke up on the point.
Mainly, the beach eroded in great ridges
until ground cover belted it back. A pleasure dome
was dismantled, certain fashions

of dress and of love. History builds to last,
crumbles to last, shakes off its dust
under the delicate excavating brush—to last.

Built above the beach was a colossus,
humped and strutted and roaring with many voices.
Winds chased through it screeching and then
it stood silent. People flocked to it, entered it,
and through not lost, screamed as if tortured.
I am joking. There was a roller coaster
of some note and no small size. Where did it go?
Ah, yes, lost in the coral make-up
of that teetering lover who walked beside me,
tired of my harangue, the persuasive underlove
that wanted to rise to the lips, those lips
colored by fuming street lamps.

Young, my parents drove out from a distant city,
though tawny hills medallioned with oak.
I have seen their worn postcards of the town,
a tide pool of neighborhoods mantled around
by semi-wilderness and orange groves.
Missiles came to squat above our house
on a benchmarked hill, turned obsolete,
and floated away on flatbeds, ruptured patios in their places.
We, too, left that house that heard,
in every lath and windowpane, the industry of phosphorus,
grinding out the waves in the late darkness.
My parents—all of us—have come and gone and left
no ghosts here, and that is our good fortune,
to give it all to the ocean, the troubled sleeper.

Carnegie-Mellon Poetry

1975
The Living and the Dead, Ann Hayes
In the Face of Descent, T. Alan Broughton

1976
The Week the Dirigible Came, Jay Meek
Full of Lust and Good Usage, Stephen Dunn

1977
*How I Escaped from the Labyrinth
and Other Poems*, Philip Dacey
The Lady from the Dark Green Hills, Jim Hall
For Luck: Poems 1962-1977, H. L. Van Brunt
By The Wreckmaster's Cottage, Paula Rankin

1978
New and Selected Poems, James Bertolino
The Sun Fetcher, Michael Dennis Browne
A Circus of Needs, Stephen Dunn
The Crowd Inside, Elizabeth Libbey

1979
Paying Back the Sea, Philip Dow
Swimmer in the Rain, Robert Wallace
Far from Home, T. Alan Broughton
The Room Where Summer Ends, Peter Cooley
No Ordinary World, Mekeel McBride

1980
*And the Man Who Was Traveling
Never Got Home*, H. L. Van Brunt
Drawing on the Walls, Jay Meek
The Yellow House on the Corner, Rita Dove
The 8-Step Grapevine, Dara Wier
The Mating Reflex, Jim Hall

1981
A Little Faith, John Skoyles
Augers, Paula Rankin

Walking Home from the Icehouse, Vern Rutsala
Work and Love, Stephen Dunn
The Rote Walker, Mark Jarman
Morocco Journal, Richard Harteis
Songs of a Returning Soul, Elizabeth Libbey

1982
The Granary, Kim R. Stafford
Calling the Dead, C. G. Hanzlicek
Dreams Before Sleep, T. Alan Broughton
Sorting it Out, Anne S. Perlman
*Love is Not a Consolation; It
 Is a Light*, Primus St. John

1983
*The Going Under of the
 Evening Land*, Mekeel McBride
Museum, Rita Dove
Air and Salt, Eve Shelnutt
Nightseasons, Peter Cooley

1984
Falling From Stardom, Jonathan Holden
Miracle Mile, Ed Ochester
Girlfriends and Wives, Robert Wallace
Earthly Purposes, Jay Meek
Not Dancing, Stephen Dunn
The Man in the Middle, Gregory Djanikian
A Heart Out of This World, David James
All You Have in Common, Dara Wier

1985
Smoke From the Fires, Michael Dennis Browne
*Full of Lust and
 Good Usage*, Stephen Dunn (2nd edition)
Far and Away, Mark Jarman
Anniversary of the Air, Michael Waters
To the House Ghost, Paula Rankin
Midwinter Transport, Anne Bromley